A Bible Study in My House?

A BIBLE STUDY IN MY HOUSE?

A Guide for Home Bible Studies

By
David and Sue Burnham

MOODY PRESS
CHICAGO

Printed in the United States of America

Contents

1

A BIBLE STUDY IN MY HOUSE?

Nearly everyone who has considered beginning a home Bible study has had feelings of being inadequate. "I just couldn't do it." Or, "I don't have the background." It is because this concern is so natural that this booklet has been put together. By sharing a few principles and experiences, it is our desire to encourage you to try. You can do it! Begin by asking for the Lord's help. You can pray and ask for the Lord's guidance and direction. Tell Him about your plans, why you want to start such a study, and whom you hope to reach. Tell Him about your fears, your ideas, your hopes; ask for His leading.

THE
FARTHEST THING FROM
THEIR MINDS

Gloria and Bill "had it made" by the time they were forty. Bill's phenomenal success in business made possible a big house in the heart of the "right" residential section, two expensive cars, children in private schools, winters in the Caribbean, and April in Paris. Gloria and Bill had everything that people think brings happiness. There was only one problem. They weren't happy. They were miserable. They felt empty.

Their materialistic victories were hollow.

So they started talking to each other and to their friends about the "meaning of life." They

GLORIA and BILL had it made,
but they weren't happy.

looked at various religious philosophies. They examined the lifestyle here and in other countries. But nothing seemed to answer their search for meaning. One day a friend invited them to attend a home Bible study. At first they refused, saying they simply didn't have time for any new activities. Several months later, they decided to give it a try. "Probably a bunch of nuts," Bill said, "but we can always cut out early."

Instead of "cutting out early," Bill and Gloria were the last to leave. They both found themselves strangely exhilarated from what they read in God's Word. Instead of more questions, they began discovering answers. Man did have a purpose for living.

The
vacuum in their lives
was
God-shaped.

Through God's Word, they discovered that the vacuum in their lives was "God-shaped." They had been trying to stuff that vacuum with cars, houses, vacations, and other things. But the only "thing" that could fill the emptiness was Jesus Christ.

Gloria and Bill discovered **who they were** by discovering Jesus Christ and **who He is,** through a home Bible study.

GLORIA
AND BILL'S
STORY
COULD BE YOURS

Once Gloria and Bill found Christ through a
Bible study, the desire grew in their hearts to
share the Good News with their friends. The
most natural way to them was—a home Bible
study. Almost everyone who discovers Christ
in this way has thought about having a Bible
study at home. It all comes from a sincere
heart-burning desire to share God's Word with
a friend.

Frankly, that is most of what it takes for a
great home Bible study program.

THERE'S NO PLACE LIKE HOME

The earliest Christians knew that one of the best places to share God's Word with friends is in the home.

In Acts 5:42, the Bible talks about the apostles teaching and preaching Jesus Christ in every house. We know Paul taught publicly and house to house (Ac 20:20). We know that churches were established in homes (Ac 10), and that Lydia's house became the first church in Philippi (Ac 16).

With this as a biblical background, there are several reasons that home Bible studies make sense in the twentieth century, too:

- The home is a warm, accepting environment.
- The home is "neutral ground" for new believers and non-believers.
- The home atmosphere encourages free expression and questions.
- The home keeps the group small enough to stay personally effective.

WHAT CAN
HOME BIBLE STUDIES
REALLY
ACCOMPLISH?

If you are not fully convinced by now, just look at a list of what a home Bible study program might do:

- Lead friends to a personal knowledge of Jesus Christ
- Undergird believers with more knowledge of their faith in Christ
- Help reassess attitudes in the light of the judgment of authoritative Scripture
- Assure better understanding of difficult passages
- Strengthen the church in meaningful small group fellowship
- Provide opportunities to actively serve Christ
- Help in learning to share Christ more effectively

The home Bible
study
is a tool.

Why a Bible study? The home Bible study is an evangelistic tool to bring people to a personal knowledge of Jesus Christ, to achieve growth for the believer and to provide meaningful fellowship.

The apostle Paul reminded Timothy, "the holy scriptures ... are able to make thee wise unto salvation through faith which is in Christ Jesus. All scripture is given by inspiration of God, and is profitable for doctrine, for reproof, for correction, for instruction in righteousness, that the man of God may be perfect, thoroughly furnished unto all good works" (2 Timothy 3:15-17).

Paul makes it pretty simple. You learn the Bible so that you become wise enough to accept God's salvation by putting your trust in Christ. The whole Bible—every bit of it, says Paul—was given to us by the inspiration of God. And the Bible is useful to teach us what is true and what is wrong in our lives. It straightens us out and helps us do the right thing. It is God's way of preparing us in every area for every situation so we can be equipped for every good work.

2

THREE STEPS TO STUDYING THE BIBLE

What does it mean?

There are probably as many different ways to study the Bible as there are people. But one we have found rewarding is asking these three questions.

1. What Does It Say?

Gather facts within a particular passage.

2. What Does It Mean?

Investigate what the passage says and arrive at a conclusion as to what it means.

3. How Does It Apply to Me?

Apply the truth of the passage personally.

One of the nicest things about this three-step study is that it promotes thorough discussion by the group through asking questions. Members are not *told* what the Bible says; they're *asked*. Together, the group discovers the facts and the meaning of the Scriptures, and each member *expresses some personal* application. The authority of the group then becomes the Bible, not an individual.

How does it work? Well, let us just take John 1 as an example.

1. What does John 1 say?

What have you learned from this Scripture? What, where, when, how? What is the main theme? You will discover how easy it is to gather all the facts about Jesus.

2. What does John 1 mean?

What did John mean by this? How is this idea related to the passage? How would you feel? If the facts of the life of Jesus Christ are gathered together, what do you conclude about Him? Is He God?

3. How does John 1 apply to me?

Although this passage is explored by the group, each person must apply the Scripture (through the power of the Holy Spirit) to his own life. The question might be asked, "How can I know more about Jesus Christ?" Frankly, it is too general to say, "I'll read my Bible more." A better, more specific application could be, "Because I want to know more about Him, I'll read my Bible for fifteen minutes every morning. I'll read it when things are quiet, so that I can concentrate better." John 1 might also apply to someone's obedience to God, or attitudes, or responsibilities. What needs a change? What should I do now? What do I need to do in the future?

You will find that this three-step method can be a big help in learning and sharing in a group. It takes the burden from one member trying to do all the teaching and to answer all the questions. It helps promote not only good discussion but good listening.

And you will find that a real trust grows between people when experiences and feelings are shared without condemnation from others. (The Scriptures do all the reproving that is necessary.)

Promoting good
discussion
and
good listening

3

LET'S
GET STARTED!

Let's get
some leaders.

OK. Let's get organized! Where do we get group leaders? (Home Bible study leaders will be referred to as "group leaders.") Well, it can happen several ways. Leaders can be contacted by the pastor. Or a leader may start the ball rolling by talking to the pastor about the need for a home Bible study within the church.

The pastor may train leaders by having a one-and-a-half-hour session each week for seven weeks, using the chapters in this book as topics. Each leader gets practice by leading the training group in a three-step Bible study of a selected scripture passage. After the session, the pastor may privately evaluate the leader on the following:

- Listening closely
- Keeping on the track
- Encouraging everybody to participate
- Organizing time properly
- Wording questions clearly

After the seven-week training session is finished, home Bible studies should be started. Church membership can be divided into zones or neighborhoods. Usually one of the members in each zone will offer his home for the beginning study. If there are enough leaders, there can be women's daytime studies and couples' evening studies.

Each week the pastor meets with the leaders and discusses the particular chapter the leader will use. This meeting not only serves to expand the dimensions of the Scripture but the leaders receive encouragement as well as have an opportunity to discuss problems and share prayer requests.

Once believers begin growing in God's Word and obeying Him, the church body will feel a new "charge of electricity."

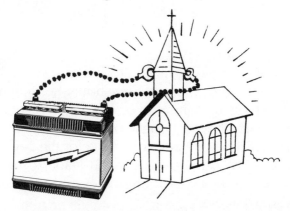

As Albert Wollen says, "Bible studies can restore deep spiritual fellowship to the heart of the church. Personality problems and church rifts will be healed and cliques eliminated."

ONCE IT GETS STARTED, IT'S CONTAGIOUS!

As enthusiasm grows for home Bible studies (and it almost always happens this way), several experienced group leaders may be asked by the pastor to help in the training and planning sessions for other leaders.

Soon you will find the need for Bible studies for those who are not church members. One of the best ways to start such a group is to have an experienced Bible leader (not the hostess) bring up the subject at a coffee or dinner. A sample study of a few verses and questions can be presented. If there is interest, the people can decide where and when a Bible study should be. Right there and then a new study can be born! There can be Bible studies by all kinds of groups, including families, singles, teenagers, senior citizens, prisoners, and workers on lunch break.

One of the purposes of reaching into the community with Bible studies is to bridge the gap between the church and the unchurched. New converts will come to church out of all sorts of nooks and crannies—from all walks of life.

4

QUALIFICATIONS FOR LEADERS

A group leader must have the following qualifications:

- Know the Lord Jesus Christ as his own personal Saviour, and be able to give a brief testimony of explanation
- Have Christ-centered values and the evidence of a new nature
- Have a personal prayer life
- Be yielded to the power of the Holy Spirit
- Study the Bible and live by it daily
- Believe confidently in the power of the inspired Word of God

A confident leader is a must.

An advanced Bible background certainly is not necessary for each leader, but commitment to **regular** study and to live by the Scriptures daily is essential.

Confidence is a must. And the leader is confident when—and only when—his confidence is grounded in the power of the inspired Word of God. That is why a pastor may suggest certain courses of Bible study for the leader's growth and knowledge. Weekly attendance at the Bible study training sessions is a must, even for the most advanced leaders.

Of course, it goes without saying that each leader must agree and cooperate with the design of the Bible study program.

DON'T STUMBLE OVER
A LEADER'S EGO!

Being a leader is not as glamorous as it may
sound. There will be many difficult moments.
A leader must deal with a whole spectrum of
personalities and needs. That is why a leader
must be stable and mature enough to deal with
various situations. The leader is not a preacher.
He is a guide that helps the group discover the
truth **together.** He cannot allow his own ego to
get in the way; he must not allow himself to
dominate the conversation or to come on as
the authority with all the answers. When a
leader simply shares insights and applications

27

(keeping his own needs in the background), a group benefits. A Christ-conscious leader will be sensitive to the needs of each member. He will have the character which reflects genuineness, and a warmth that is not possessive of the group's admiration and attention.

5

BACK TO BASICS

It is not a bad idea to read these basics aloud at the beginning of a Bible study series. Maybe you should even **reread** items 6-9 periodically.

1. Let's all talk about it.

The three steps to Bible study (what does it say, what does it mean, how does it apply to me) are designed to stimulate group discussion.

2. We don't need a preacher. We need a guide!

No one (and that means **no one**) teaches the class, preaches or lectures; the leader **guides** the discussion.

3. Newcomers are welcome.

Because each study discovers what a certain passage says, a newcomer, with or without Bible background, can come and can participate.

4. Watch the words!

Be extra careful of terminology. A good idea is to define words from the dictionary and to refrain from using an expression not found in the passage of Scripture being studied. There really should not be any need to read from books and other commentaries during the study. Various translations of the Bible, an English dictionary, and a discussion guide, if desired, are all you need.*

---

*See *John.' Told with Love* and *Fascinating Women* by David Burnham and Sue Burnham (Chicago: Moody Press, 1975) for discussion guides that follow the methods used in this book.

5. Play "change the discussion leader."

It is perfectly all right to change discussion leaders (not the group leader) at any time. The person who leads by asking questions learns the most and presents new ideas.

6. Don't wander around, or you will get lost.

Stick to the Bible passage under discussion. However, as the group proceeds, some referral back to preceding portions of the particular book under discussion is beneficial.

7. Stay on target!

It is tempting (especially in group discussions) to digress. Sharing is important, but long discussions on other subjects can

lead away from the main points of the passage. So avoid tangents. Don't fall prey to extraneous facts. And, perhaps most important of all, don't discuss specific **churches or pastors.**

8. Everybody takes part!

Encourage each member to get involved in discussion. That means some members must be encouraged to start talking. Others should stop talking and listen.

Lateness
is rudeness
to others.

9. Begin and end on time!

Nothing is more frustrating than a meeting that starts late and then drags on and on. Once chronic stragglers find you are going to start on time, they will be there. So begin **and end** the study at the agreed time. One hour is usually the right amount of time to cover the main points in each section and present a conclusion.

10. Decide how many weeks the study will last.

Decide on a definite period of time to cover a particular book or topic. Then, when the study is completed, the group can decide when the next series of studies should begin. The pastor can help by suggesting starting and stopping points. As you might expect, studies are usually suspended during summer and holiday weeks.

11. Meet in one home or rotate.

Some Bible studies meet in the same home each week; others, especially in neighborhood studies, meet in different homes. The important point, however, is not where you meet but the feeling of the friendly, cordial atmosphere. Sometimes babysitting is provided with each mother sharing in the expenses and taking her turn in transporting the sitter.

12. Total duration is one and one-half hours weekly.

The first half hour of the Bible study can be used to serve refreshments, to make sure all have arrived and to handle the chit-chat. Different members of the study may volunteer to bring refreshments (which should be kept simple).

6

YOU KNEW THERE HAD TO BE SPECIAL PROBLEMS!

The following are a few suggestions for coping with some problems which may arise.

1. The Overtalkative: Group Enemy No. 1

Domination of discussion by a class member is probably the No. 1 killer of small Bible studies. If one person persists in dominating the discussion, the leader must ask if anyone else has something to say. If the compulsive talker continues, the leader must take him aside and discuss the prob-

Watch out for the compulsive talker.

lem. Sometimes asking the talker to help in encouraging others to participate can help. The rule of thumb is to deal with the problem firmly, but with love.

2. Wrong Answers

When someone gives an incorrect answer, our first tendency is to jump in with both feet and say, "You are wrong." Well, the person may be wrong, but so is our response. Instead, repeat the question to the group and ask for other opinions. If the answer is still not correct, ask, "Where in the Scriptures do you find your answer?" Again, handle wrong answers with love.

She took off in
all directions.

3. Going Off On A Tangent

If the discussion gets sidetracked from the main issue, the leader can get back to the topic by repeating the last question. Or by asking for the next Scripture to be read. You may also suggest that those who are interested in this tangent stay after the study and discuss it.

4. **Dealing With Cultists**

   If the intention of the "cultist" is to seek scriptural truth and not to use the Bible study as a launching pad for some unscriptural doctrines, then have no qualms about inviting him to your study. If a cultist (or anyone who promotes an unscriptural doctrine) persists in using the group to pressure people into accepting these ideas, the leader must ask him to leave. It seems hard, yet it is the only way a group can continue to know and apply the truth from the Bible.

5. **Sharing, Not Confessing**

   Sharing personal experiences of growing in Christian maturity benefits the group. However, confessing all the intimate details to the whole group should be discouraged. If an individual has personal problems, the leader can offer personal counseling.

6. Planning, Patience and Persistence

To have a good, rewarding Bible study takes planning, a spirit of patience, and persistence. The beginning may be small; but, if you persist and depend upon the Holy Spirit's work, growth will come. When a problem pops up, turn it over to the Lord in prayer. Adding a prayer partner can help. And just remember, every Bible study that ever started had some problems. But God brings the increase.

7

SPECIAL MEETINGS FOR SPECIAL OCCASIONS

There are at least four times during the year when special meetings can be planned to meet special needs.

FALL KICKOFF

Fall is a great time to plan a Bible Study Kickoff. The pastor or chairman of Bible studies can invite leaders (and co-leaders) to an initial session. This meeting, lasting about two hours, includes the following:

A good kickoff means a lot to the way a game goes.

- Introduction of leaders
- Time and place of Bible studies
- Calendar of events
- Summary of leader's responsibility
- Scriptural challenge by an experienced, eager, enthusiastic Bible leader

This informational kickoff can be a breakfast, luncheon, tea, or evening dessert and can be held in the fellowship hall of the church or any centrally located meeting place. Previous to the kickoff, the chairman and area coordinators should type up the calendar of events, all Bible leader names, telephone numbers, place and day of study. If the Bible study is being organized for church members, the name of each member should be typed on a card and the cards arranged according to zones. Area coordinators can give each group Bible study leader the names and addresses of members he should contact.

AFTER EIGHT TO TEN WEEKS

After eight to ten weeks of Bible study, all Bible leaders, members of other studies, and friends can be invited to a special meeting. Women might enjoy a luncheon; men, a breakfast. An evening dessert might also be appropriate.

This meeting is primarily an **evangelistic outreach**. A challenging, clear message from God's Word can be presented along with a definite opportunity to make a decision for Christ. It is helpful for all study members to look beyond their own study and see that they are part of something a whole lot bigger.

Chairmen of Bible studies and area coordinators can plan this event. Tickets can be sold in Bible studies a few weeks in advance. Name tags should be available at the meeting. The pastor can suggest speakers. Christian women's clubs and Christian businessmen's associations are good sources for speakers.

Christmas is a
perfect time
to tell
Christ's story.

CHRISTMAS GET-TOGETHERS

Christmas coffees, desserts, etc. are a good opportunity for Bible study members to invite friends and neighbors to hear the Christmas story. It is a good idea to make the invitation in writing, since this is a very busy time of the year. An "outside" Bible leader can present the Christmas challenge, including the story of Christmas and a personal testimony. Perhaps a talented member of the study group could write about the Christmas challenge; maybe other leaders or the pastor might have suggestions for how best to use these Christmas get-togethers. But whatever you do, this is the perfect season for telling not only the story of Christ but what it means to our lives. A holiday treat can be served wherever it seems appropriate, and guests can be invited to the next regular meeting of the weekly Bible study.

TO
GOD
BE THE
GLORY!

SPRING—A SPRINGBOARD

In the spring, Bible study leaders and members can be invited to a bring-your-own informal salad luncheon or dinner—day session from 10 A.M. to 2 P.M., or evening session from 7 to 10 P.M., if preferred. The primary purpose is sharing experiences in Christian growth and encouraging new believers. It is also a chance for challenging Bible study group members to become Bible leaders in their own neighborhoods. Christian books should be available; three-minute book reports could be presented. This program should be centered around personal testimonies from people who have been contacted several weeks in advance. Be careful—churches, denominations, or people should not be praised in the testimony. **The testimony should glorify Jesus Christ.**

There may be music or a special speaker. It is up to you and certainly not necessary. The Bible leaders' training program should be announced at this meeting. It is also very helpful if the training program can be completed before the leaders scatter in the summertime.

SUMMARY CALENDAR OF
SPECIAL OCCASIONS

SEPTEMBER
Bible study kickoff for leaders

NOVEMBER
Luncheon or dinner for leaders, members, and friends

DECEMBER
Holiday get-together for leaders, members, and friends

MARCH
Seminar and sharing for leaders and members

APRIL
Training session for new leaders

AND FINALLY

When God's Word is proclaimed—whether in a home Bible study, from the pulpit, or in Yankee Stadium—we know the lasting work is not done by us. It is done in the hearts of individuals by the Holy Spirit of God.

"For the word of God is living, and powerful, and sharper than any two-edged sword, piercing even to the dividing asunder of soul and spirit, and of the joints, and marrow, and is a discerner of the thoughts and intents of the heart" (Hebrews 4:12).